Table of Contents

Technique is found on pages 2-3, 6-7, 10, 14, 16, 18, 23, 27,

UNIT 1   Review of 10 basic techniques; review of sixteenth-note patterns; New: ♫ mixed with ♪ and ♪; review of scales, cadences, triads and inversions, and arpeggios, Circle of Fifths; *tremolo; leggero; più mosso; accelerando* 2-9

UNIT 2   Introducing the other two pedals; introduction to augmented triads; review of diminished triads and Circle of Fifths; new ways to practice arpeggios; *grazioso; scherzando; sostenuto* 10-15

UNIT 3   Finger independence; review of the Baroque era and trills; introduction to more ornaments; *appoggiaturas;* mordents 16-21

UNIT 4   The Sonatina and the Classical Era; practice techniques 22-25

UNIT 5   ♫; review of intervals and finger independence; introduction to major seventh chords (M7), minor seventh chords (m7), and diminished seventh chords (dim7); *portato; meno* 26-33

UNIT 6   Voicing; review of sequences; *tranquillo; con brio; marcato* 34-40

UNIT 7   The Romantic Era; review of balance between the hands and voicing 41-44

UNIT 8   Seven touch releases; introduction to a new touch release: hammer stroke/woodpecker 45-54

UNIT 9   The Key of E♭ major: scale, cadence, triads and inversions, arpeggio; assymetrical rhythms and changing time signatures; *rubato* 55-61

UNIT 10 The Key of C minor: 3 forms of C minor scale, cadence, arpeggio; *ballade; agitato; animato* 62-69

Music Dictionary 70-71

Certificate of Achievement 72

Production: Frank J. Hackinson
Production Coordinators: Peggy Gallagher and Philip Groeber
Editors: Edwin McLean and Peggy Gallagher
Art Direction: Andi Whitmer – in collaboration with Helen Marlais
Cover Illustration: ©2013 Susan Hellard/Arena
Interior Illustrations: ©2013 Teresa Robertson/Arena
Cover and Interior Illustration Concepts: Helen Marlais
Engraving: Tempo Music Press, Inc.
Printer: Tempo Music Press, Inc.

10 Basic Techniques – REVIEW

1. POSTURE

- Sit tall and long. Be aware of the four natural curves of your spine and how your head is balanced on top of the spine.

- Let your neck and shoulders be free.

- Your feet should be flat on the floor for balance.

- Your torso and forearms should be balanced over the keys that you play. Lean forward into the keys for power.

2. ARM WEIGHT

Drop your forearm and wrist at the same time to the bottom of the keys. Your hand, arm, wrist, and forearm move as one playing unit. Think of a strong bridge as you play, and your sound will be confident and beautiful.

good!

- * Imagine a downhill skier who was told not to move his knees up and down naturally when skiing down a mountain. He wouldn't be able to go very far! The same is true for pianists—let your wrists and forearms drop naturally to the bottom of the keys, and then release your muscles by rolling your wrists slightly forward. This will result in a beautiful sound and gesture.

3. STRONG FINGERS

Experiment with different sounds produced by strong fingers. If you play with strong fingertips, you will create a brilliant sound. If you desire a more mellow, singing sound, play more on the fleshy pads of your fingers. Play a scale twice, changing the place on your fingers that you make contact with the keys. How do the two scales sound different?

4. WEIGHT TRANSFER

Keep in mind that when playing, your fingers, hands, wrist, and arms should move together, at the same time, as one playing unit. Imagine a strong bridge from your shoulder to your fingertips. Learning to transfer, or shift, your weight from one finger to the next will help you play with a beautiful and even sound because weight transfer makes each finger of the hand feel like it is the same length.

- * Imagine a surfer who tried to surf with his legs moving in one direction and his arms moving in another direction. The surfer wouldn't be able to stay up on the surfboard! The same is true for pianists – let your arms, wrists, and fingers move together at the same time so that your playing is effortless, the sound is beautiful, and your motions are controlled and easy.

not good!

FJH2178

5. FLEXIBLE WRISTS

Often piano music must be played with strong hands, wrists, and forearms as one playing unit. At other times, the wrists need to be flexible. Breathe with your wrists to create even passagework and good shaping of phrases and motives. Your wrists should move along with your forearms for tension-free playing.

   * Imagine a runner who always ran without moving his ankles. The runner wouldn't be able to go far or fast! The same is true for pianists — let your arms and wrists move naturally so that you play with well-coordinated motion.

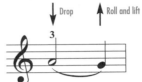

6. TWO-NOTE SLURS

You are probably an expert by now on these!
Remember to: drop, roll, and lift.

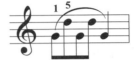

7. ROTATION

Rotation is just like turning a key in a lock, rock your hand, wrist, and forearm from side to side. Never stretch or reach for any keys but instead use weight transfer to move.

8. BALANCE BETWEEN THE HANDS

Listening to and bringing out the hand that has the melody makes you a sensitive musician!

   * Imagine a rowing team rowing a boat in a competition. The rowing team in the boat is like a melody in music, and the water underneath them is like the harmony in music.

9. PEDALING

Chopin once said: "The pedal is the soul of the piano." Let your ear be your guide when using the pedal. Practice without the pedal to be sure of your sound, evenness in playing, and *legato* articulation. Then add the pedal for the desired sound effect.

10. SCALES, CADENCES, TRIADS and INVERSIONS, ARPEGGIOS

These techniques are the foundation for your piano playing. Practice these every day to be a fine pianist and musician.

For extra technique practice, use *Energize Your Fingers Every Day*™, Book 5, *Play Your Scales and Chords Every Day*®, Books 5-7, and *Succeeding with the Masters*® & *The Festival Collection*®: *Etudes with Technique*, Books 3 and 4.

Review of Sixteenth-Note Patterns

Tap and count aloud. ♩ = ca. 88

Triplets Mixed with Sixteenth Notes

Look at triplets ♪♪♪ with ♩, ♪, and ♪
Clap and count aloud. ♩ = ca. 88. Feel the main pulse throughout.

Grand Central Station

by Timothy Brown

Vivo (♩ = ca. 96)

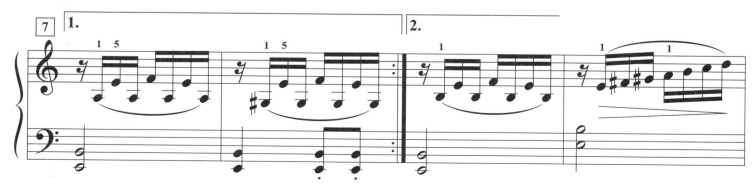

4

FJH2178

* *tremolo*—rapidly play the 2 notes back and forth.

Technique with Beethoven

• Here's a daily warm-up you can use that will help you be a terrific pianist!

1. **Play a two-octave major scale.** $\quad$ = 72, $\quad$ = 96, $\quad$ = _____.
your choice

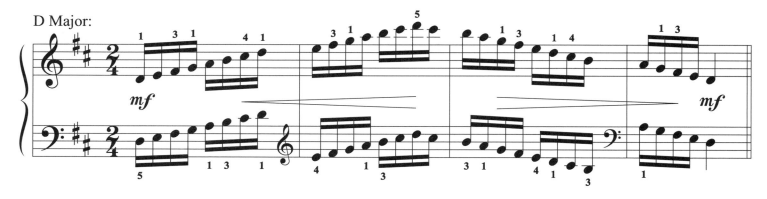

2. **Then play the cadence.**
• This is an "authentic" cadence because it ends with a dominant 7th chord leading to the tonic.

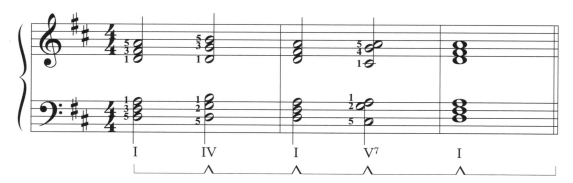

Beethoven says: Can you bring out the top note of the chords in the cadence? This means to **voice** the melody. You'll learn more about this later.

3. Next play the triads and inversions.

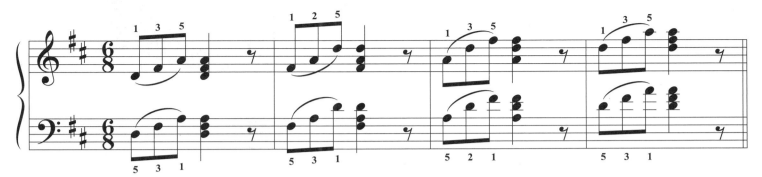

4. Finally, play a two-octave arpeggio.

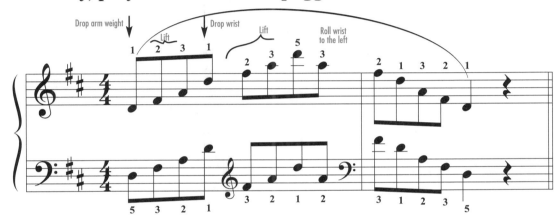

 Beethoven says: • Imagine your five fingers are friends. Don't separate and straighten your fingers.

• Don't stretch or reach for any key. Instead, use weight transfer and roll your wrist from one finger to the next.

• As soon as your thumb plays, move it along and watch that it doesn't stick out or stay under the palm.

• The thumb must stay close to the other fingers, and let it relax.

Check off the following major keys (1 key every week is a good plan.)

C _____   G _____   D _____   A _____   E _____

B _____   F♯ _____   C♯ _____   A♭ _____

E♭ _____   B♭ _____   F _____

(Practice in the Circle of Fifths.)

In Flight
by Mary Leaf

CD 5/6 • MIDI 3

FJH2178

Technique with Chopin
Introducing the other two pedals

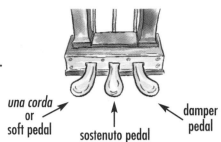

- The soft pedal or *una corda* not only makes the piano quieter, but it also changes the sound.
- The *sostenuto* pedal is used for advanced works. It sustains only the tones sounded by the keys already being depressed.
- These pedals work best on grand pianos.

una corda or soft pedal → sostenuto pedal → damper pedal

Learning Augmented Triads

Chopin says:

To build an augmented (aug.) triad, raise the 5th of a major triad one half step. The sound has a "questioning" or "surprising" quality.

raised fifth

- You have already learned diminished triads in Grade 4.
- Play the following triads. Once you begin, continue in the Circle of Fifths.

* Use fingers 1-3-5 for all triads.

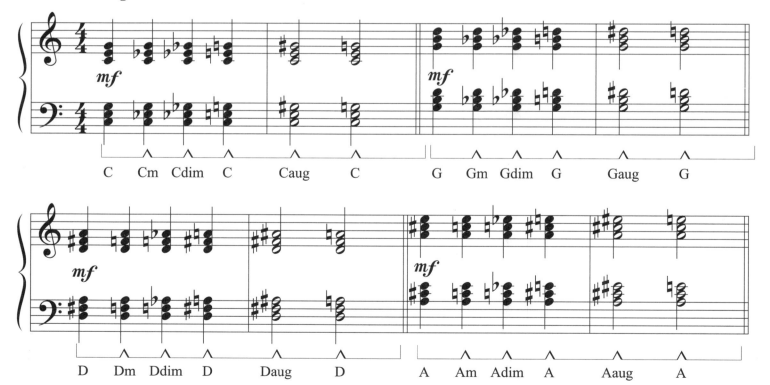

(Note to teachers: A simple explanation of the two other pedals (besides the damper pedal) will be fine. If a student has a grand piano, have them experiment with the soft pedal with the triads on this page.)

There are three diminished triads in this piece.
In root position, they are built with stacked minor 3rds:

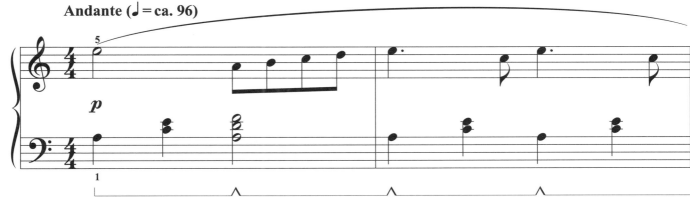

root position   root position (2nd inversion)   root position (2nd inversion)

- Find and play them.

Theme from Sleeping Beauty

by Pyotr Ilyich Tchaikovsky
1840-1893, Russia
Arranged by Edwin McLean

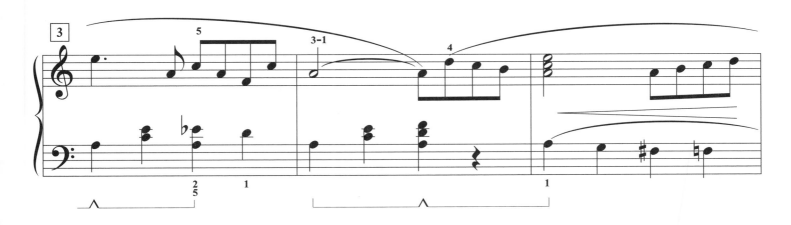

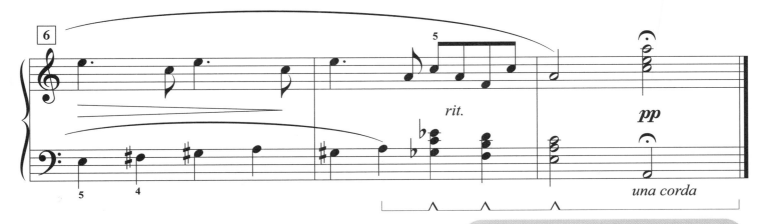

After playing, ask yourself:
- Did I play with a singing tone?
- Did I play each phrase with a phrase goal (high point of the phrase)?

Before playing:

• Find and play the two augmented triads.

The Young Prince and The Young Princess

from *Scheherazade*
by Nikolai Rimsky-Korsakov
1844-1908, Russia
Arranged by Kevin Olson

(Note to teachers: The grace notes in measure 7 and 15 are to be played melodically, before the beat.)

FJH2178

Practicing arpeggios:

· The following exercise will make your arpeggios dazzle!

· Practice hands apart, then together, and crescendo to the highest note.

The Little Sprite

by Cornelius Gurlitt
1820-1901, Germany

Vivace molto (♩ = ca. 120)

FJH2178

Technique with J. S. Bach
Finger Independence

- Finger independence is needed when one hand has to play two lines of music at the same time.
- The music of the Baroque era (1600-1750), when J. S. Bach lived, uses finger independence.

Let's try some exercises so you can learn this important skill.

- Practice with the metronome. ♩ = ca. 72
- Practice hands apart, then hands together.
- When you drop, use your arm weight to play to the bottom of the key.

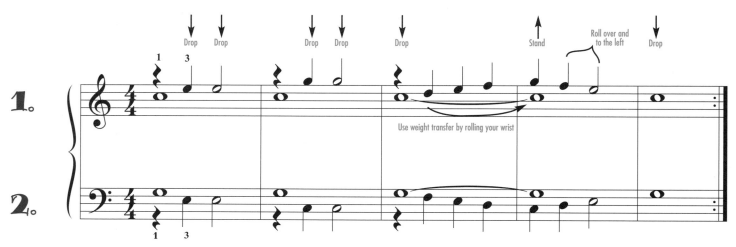

FJH2178

- Practice the L.H. until it feels natural.

Spring Awakening

by Ferdinand Beyer
1803-1863, Germany

CD 15/16 • MIDI 9

After playing, ask yourself:
- Did I hear the finger independence in the L.H.?

Technique with Mozart
Practicing Ornaments

- Ornaments are notes that decorate and fill out a musical line. Ornaments make music more expressive and grand!
- In Grade 4, you learned the trill, ⌁ or *tr*.
- Now let's learn the *appoggiatura* (ahp-pah-jah-TOO-rah).

Mozart says: You will see this ornament often in my music and in the music of other classical composers.

When you see this:  , play this:

- Notice that the small note borrows time from the second, longer note.

When you see this:  , play this:

- When the second note is a ♩, ♩, or 𝅝 note, the first small note gets HALF the value of the second note.

When you see this:  , play this:

When you see this:  , play this:

- When the second note is a ♩., the first small note gets two-thirds of the beat.

When you see this:  , play this:

- When the second note is an ♪, the notes are all ♪

Mozart says: The ornaments on this page are **upper appoggiaturas** because they start on the upper note. The *appoggiaturas* on the next page are **lower appoggiaturas** because they start on the lower note.

FJH2178

Before playing:

- There are six phrases in this piece.
  Listen to the CD to hear the forward direction.

- Find the two *appoggiaturas*. Notice how the nonharmonic tone
  resolves to the chord tone.

Minuet in C

by Wolfgang Amadeus Mozart
1756-1791, Austria

FJH2178

The Mordent

• ❧ This ornament adds brilliance to the melodic line. It is always played on the beat and goes down then back up.

Minuet in G Major

(from The Anna Magdalena Bach Notebook)
BWV Anh. 114
by Christian Petzold
1677-1733, Germany

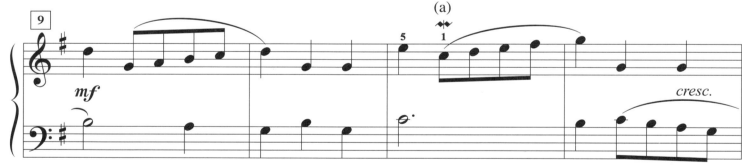

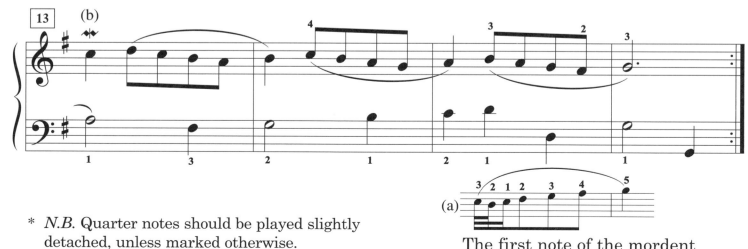

* *N.B.* Quarter notes should be played slightly detached, unless marked otherwise.

The first note of the mordent begins *on* the beat.

FJH2178

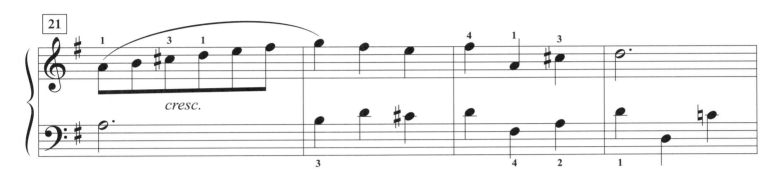

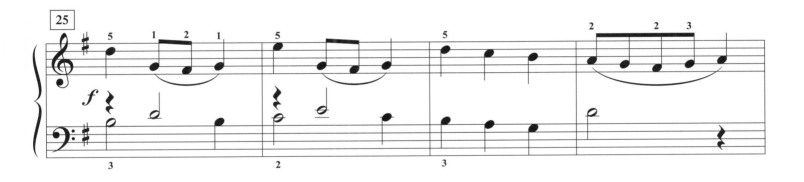

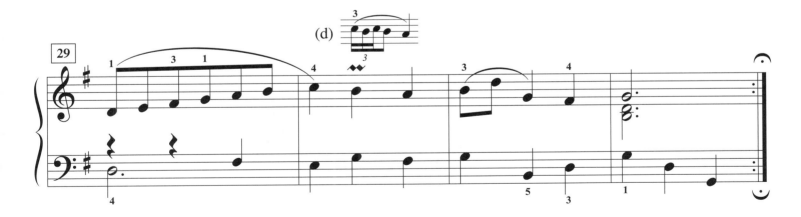

(d) Optional trill:

After playing, ask yourself:
• Were all my ornaments played on the beat?

The Sonatina

A sonatina is a "little sonata." Usually a sonata is a piece for piano, or for a solo instrument and piano. Sonatinas and sonatas were written during the Classical Era (1750-1820) by many composers including Clementi, Haydn, Mozart, and Beethoven.

Sonatinas typically have two or three movements. Each movement in a sonatina may use a different tempo, key, mood, and character, or "personality."

Pieces in the Classical era are well balanced and symmetrical. They have tuneful melodies, which means that you can easily sing them!

Look at the Roman columns below and notice their symmetry and balance. Classical composers believed in this kind of structure in their forms.

The first movement of a sonatina or sonata is typically in *sonata form*. Sonata form means that there are three sections. These are called:

EXPOSITION
- Is usually made up of two contrasting themes. Usually the first theme is in the tonic key, the second theme is in the dominant key.

- Ends with a repeat sign.

DEVELOPMENT
- Thematic material is now changed, or "developed."

RECAPITULATION
- The first theme is restated, as heard in the exposition. The main theme is in the tonic key. If the second theme is restated, it's also in the tonic key.

- A *coda* is often an ending section that is played. In Italian, coda means "tail." A *codetta* is a "little coda."

(For more sonatinas to play, see *Succeeding with the Masters*®/*The Festival Collection*® *Sonatinas*, Books 3 and 4).

Technique with Haydn

Clementi was a pianist, teacher, and composer. He was also a music publisher and piano manufacturer. Many people discussed who was a more skilled pianist and improvisor—Clementi or Mozart.

Practice Techniques:

- When learning a new piece, remember that your first goal is to play the **NOTES**, **FINGERING**, **RHYTHM**, and **ARTICULATIONS** correctly. Play short segments at a slow tempo with a warm, big sound.

- Only when you have mastered this first goal should you add the dynamics and increase the tempo.

Practice these short phrases 5 times each correctly. Play slowly and rhythmically.

The wrist and forearm play as one unit

Bounce off the G's. Don't stretch or reach but leap, using weight transfer

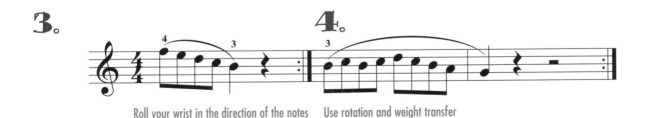

Roll your wrist in the direction of the notes   Use rotation and weight transfer

5. Alberti Bass:

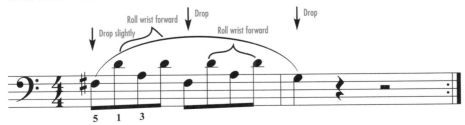

Find other short phrases in the music on p. 24 and p. 25 to practice like this.

When playing:

- The Classical Era was known for its "singing allegros." Bring out the melody over the harmony and make each phrase sing!

Sonatina

Opus 36, No. 1, Movement 1

by Muzio Clementi
1752-1832, Italy

FJH2178

This entire sonatina (movements 1, 2, and 3) is found in *The Festival Collection*®, Book 3.

A New Sixteenth-Note Rhythm Pattern

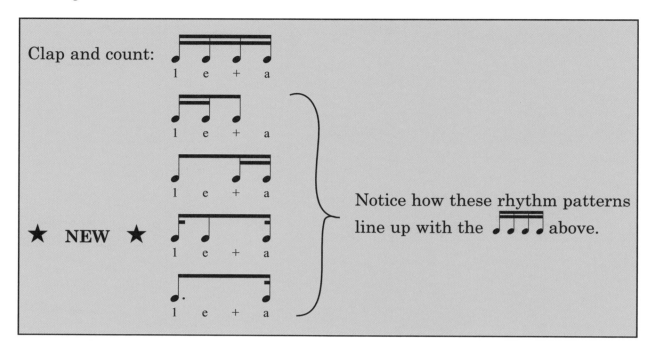

1. Tap the following patterns with your teacher, counting aloud.

2. Write in the counting. Then tap and count aloud.

* You will play a piece with this new rhythm pattern on p. 28.

Technique with Brahms
Review of Intervals (2nds through octaves)

Brahms says:
Play the following intervals using **arm rotation**. "Throw" your arm from side to side so that you don't reach or stretch for keys.

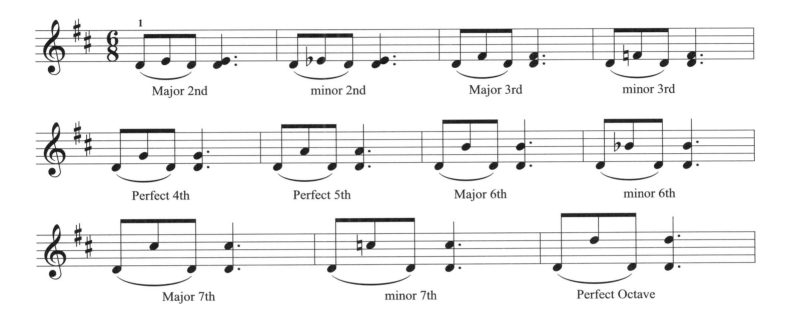

Complete each interval *above* the given note. Then play them.

Remember to use a major scale on the beginning note to figure out intervals.

- Tritones are made up of three whole steps.
- In early centuries, a tritone was considered to be very bad, but not anymore.
- It is the least stable of all intervals. (It sounds like it wants to resolve.)

Think of a tritone as an augmented 4th.

Sambalele

(Samba)

Traditional Brazilian Dance
Arranged by Timothy Brown

Happily! (♩ = ca. 72)

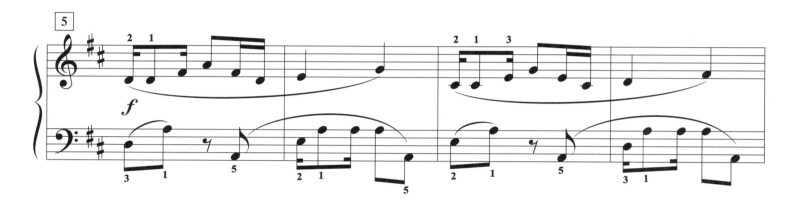

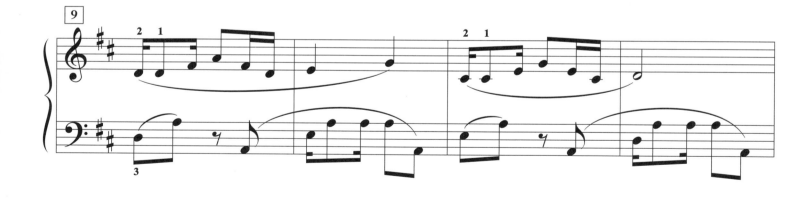

FJH2178

Review of Finger Independence

Little Romance

from *First Instruction in Piano Playing*
by Carl Czerny
1791-1857, Austria

After playing, ask yourself:
- Did I play with a singing tone?

FJH2178

Technique with Brahms

Major Seventh (M7) Chord
Minor Seventh (m7) Chord
Diminished Seventh (dim7) Chord

- Notice the difference between these chords compared to the dominant seventh (V7) chords you know.

Key of F Major:

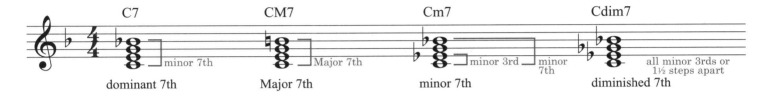

Brahms says:

As you play each chord, drop your arm weight to the bottom of the keys. Keep a strong hand arch and play on the flat side of your thumb. Listen for a sustained, singing sound. Next, **slowly** lift your weight *out of the keys* with your forearms. This **portato touch** is used for chords where you need a lush and big sound.

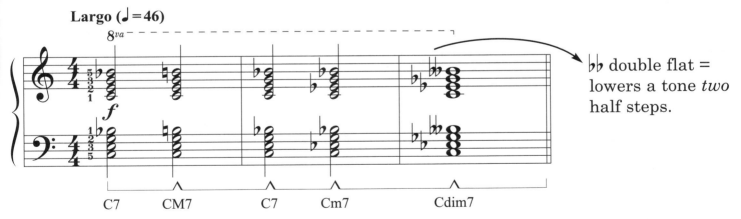

♭♭ double flat = lowers a tone *two* half steps.

Continue with the Circle of Fifths.

Technique Tip: Sit in the MIDDLE of your two hands when playing these chords.

Before playing:

- Listen to the CD recording. Block the chords and name them as you play. In which measure is there a C#dim7 chord? _____

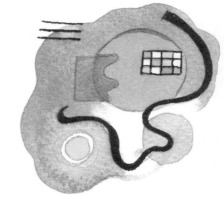

Twilight Fantasy

by Edwin McLean

 CD 30/31 • MIDI 18

Delicato; espressivo (♩ = 104)

FJH2178

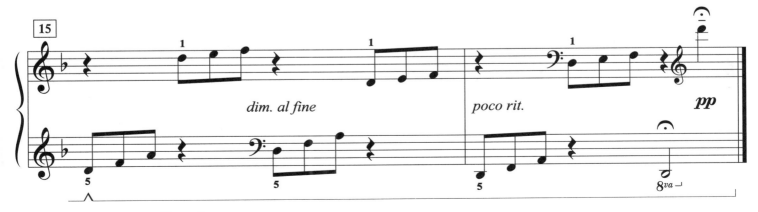

* "meno" means "less."

Technique with Chopin
Voicing

- Voicing means to bring out a melody over an accompaniment or bring out the top note of a chord. Practicing finger independence will help you learn how.

- Voicing makes the music that you play truly beautiful.

Chopin says:

Use weight transfer for this technique. Roll your wrist and forearm in the direction of the notes. Listen to bring out the melody over the inner notes by giving the fingers that play the melody more weight from the arm.

1.

2.

3.

FJH2178

Practice steps:

- Practice only the R.H. melody first, without the inner notes.
- Practice the R.H. melody with the L.H.
- Then practice the two voices in the R.H.
- Listen for a beautiful *legato*.

Indigo Dusk
by Helen Marlais

Tenderly; expressively (♩ = ca. 132)

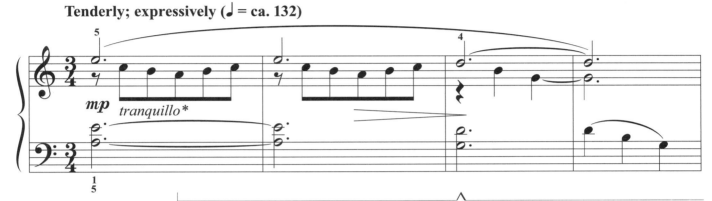

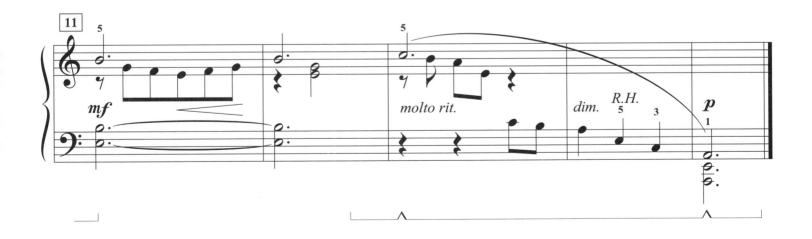

* *tranquillo*—calm, peaceful.

Canon in D

by Johann Pachelbel
1653-1706, Germany
Arranged by Timothy Brown

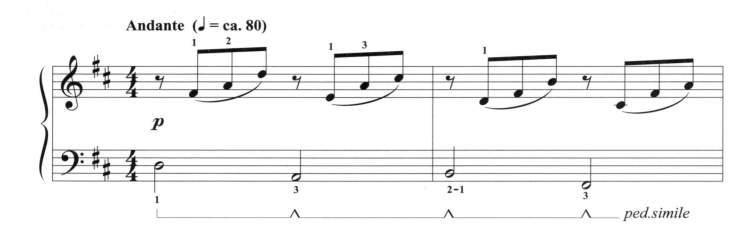

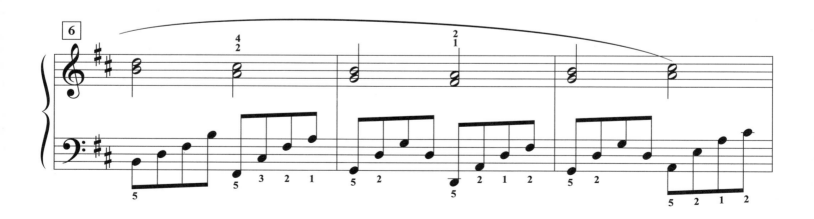

FJH2178

FJH2178

Review of Sequences

- A sequence is a phrase that is immediately repeated on a different pitch.
- Notice the sequences in measures 1 to 8.

 CD 37/38 • MIDI 22

Toccatina

by J. C. Bach and F. P. Ricci

1735-1782, Germany / 1732-1817, Italy

Con brio (with spirit)

* *marcato*—means marked, stressed.

FJH2178

The Romantic Era

CD 39 • MIDI 23

The Romantic Era came after the Classical Era. The Romantic Era lasted from around 1800-1900.

Composers were interested in nature, imagery, and feeling. This was the time of the soloist, and many famous pianists toured before captivated audiences, large and small.

Many pieces during this time had descriptive titles. Listen to the following two pieces on the CD and look at the music below.

Think about the sound and the mood of each one. Which one sounds calm and peaceful, like a garden? Which one is energetic and sounds like horn calls?

Circle the correct title for each:

This piece is: **In the Garden** or **Hunting Music**

This piece is: **In the Garden** or **Hunting Music**

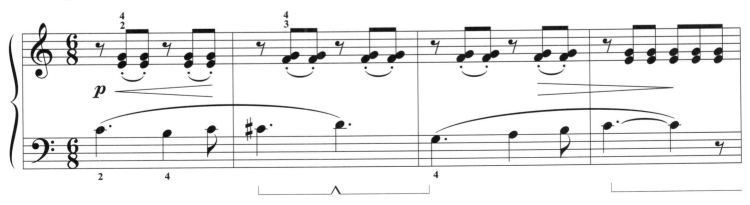

Answer: (1): Hunting Music; (2): In the Garden

When playing:

- Bring out the melody and listen to the balance between the hands.
- Notice the long Romantic phrases.

Theme from the "Unfinished" Symphony

by Franz Schubert
1797-1828, Austria
Arranged by Mary Leaf

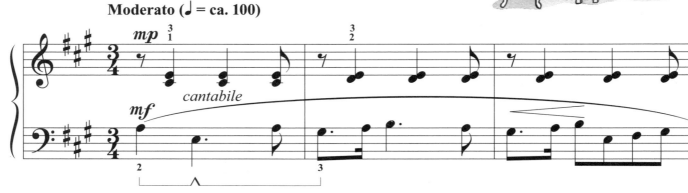

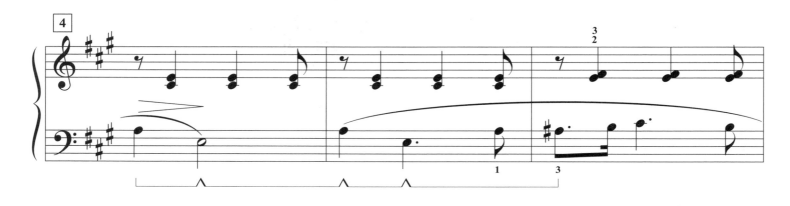

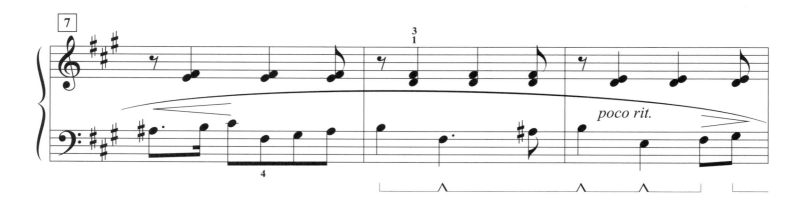

Franz Schubert (1797-1828) was born in Vienna, Austria, and lived in a one-bedroom apartment with his mother, father, and four siblings. Franz's first teacher was his brother Ignaz; his father taught him to play the violin. By the time he was thirteen he had composed songs, string quartets, and piano pieces. He also sang in the famous boys' choir of the Imperial High Chapel in Vienna. Schubert is known for many kinds of works, especially over 600 wonderful songs for voice and piano.

FJH2178

Melody

Op. 68, No. 1
by Robert Schumann
1810-1856, Germany

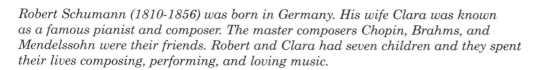

Robert Schumann (1810-1856) was born in Germany. His wife Clara was known as a famous pianist and composer. The master composers Chopin, Brahms, and Mendelssohn were their friends. Robert and Clara had seven children and they spent their lives composing, performing, and loving music.

Robert and Clara Schumann

FJH2178

Technique with Mozart
Seven Touch Releases

- The more control you have with different touches at the piano, the more you will refine your technique. In this way, you will become a fine pianist who plays in a dazzling manner and with beauty.

1. Drop and Lift

The basic gesture of dropping your arm weight to the bottom of the keys and then lifting your weight out of the keys, wrist first. Needed for two-note and three-note slurs and other phrase shapes.

Waltz
by Johannes Brahms

2. Push Off!

Arm weight is used to drop the wrist and forearm to the bottom of the key, and the wrist pushes forward quickly for a crisp, snappy sound. The sound will change depending on the quickness of the release and how far the hand is released from the keyboard.

Arabesque
by Johann Friedrich Burgmüller

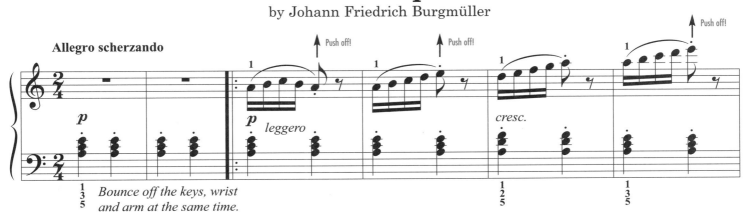

3. Kick Off!

Has a sharp attack and a short release. Your hand, wrist, and forearm form a strong bridge, and work as *one playing unit*. The wrist does not bend on the way down or on the way up. However, there is a slight release on the way up so that you do not feel any tension when you play. Often the Kick Off! has a short, sharp release, but it can also have a quieter sound. You can experiment with this important touch release in most of the pieces you play.

The Banjo
by Louis Moreau Gottschalk

4. Rebound Staccato

The hand, wrist, and forearm move downward as one playing unit. Throw your "playing unit" into the key and rebound back up, wrist first. This technique is used for *staccato* melodies and for repeated notes.

Grandmama's Waltz
by Louis Köhler

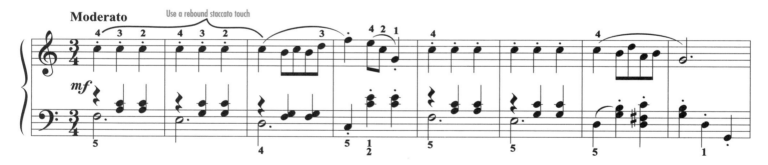

5. The "Tissue Box"

This is similar to the "Push Off" except that it has a soft attack and a gentle release. This technique is used when the music calls for a wispy, soft, special sound.

6. Portato

This is a touch and a sound between staccato and legato. Think of it as a "sticky" feel and sound. Drop your arm weight to the bottom of the keys. Then slowly push off the keys with your wrists and forearms, lifting your weight **out** of the keys. The weight of your arms should be centered over the fingers that play. Your torso and forearm shift to exactly where the chords are played on the piano.

Prelude
by Carl Czerny

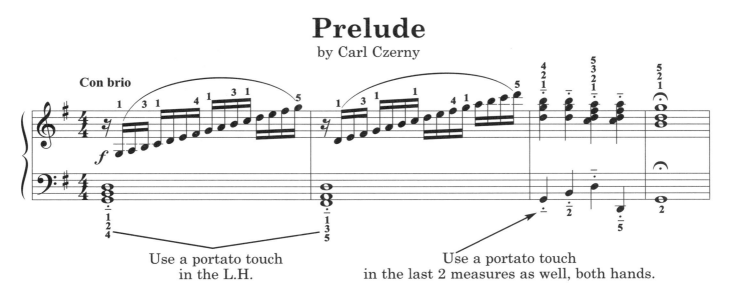

Use a portato touch
in the L.H.

Use a portato touch
in the last 2 measures as well, both hands.

7.

A NEW TOUCH RELEASE
Hammer Stroke—or "Woodpecker"

This technique is for repetitive articulations where precision and rhythmic accuracy is important. The hand is very close to the keys at all times. The technique is like that of the "Kick Off!" where the playing unit consists of the hand, wrist, and arm that play at the same time. However, the main difference is that the playing unit moves downward (like a hammer pounding or a woodpecker pecking the side of a tree) and springs slightly upward after each repetition.

Jack Frost
by Jean Louis Gobbaerts (aka Streabbog)

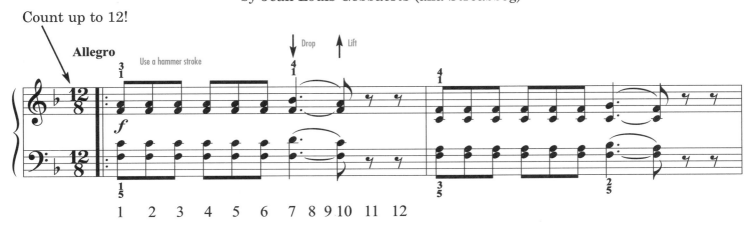

Note to teachers: Students will learn these techniques and be able to apply them to all their future pieces. Have them use the name of each technique to remember each one.

Arabesque

Opus 100, No. 2

by Johann Friedrich Burgmüller
1806-1874, Germany

Allegro scherzando (♩ = ca. 120)

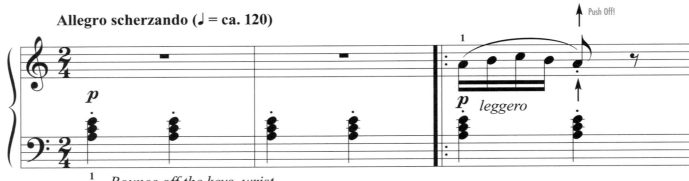

*Bounce off the keys, wrist
and arm at the same time.*

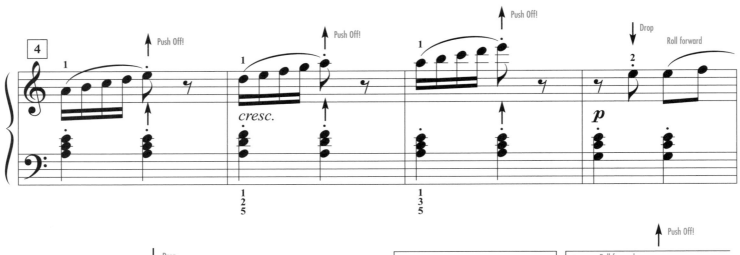

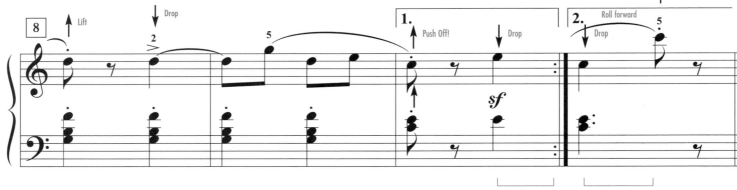

FJH2178

Louis Moreau Gottschalk (1829-1869) was the first American virtuoso/composer. He lived during the Romantic Era in New Orleans, and was inspired by Creole music and culture. He also traveled and performed in Latin America and the Caribbean. You can hear the folk themes and rhythms of these various cultures in many of his pieces. He is considered to be the first composer to truly write in an American style, and his music was very popular during his lifetime.

The Banjo
by Louis Moreau Gottschalk
1829-1869, U.S.A.
Arranged by Timothy Brown

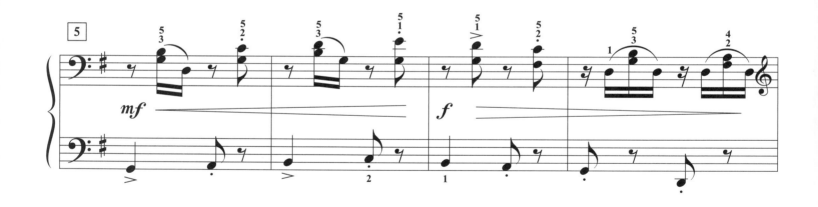

FJH2178

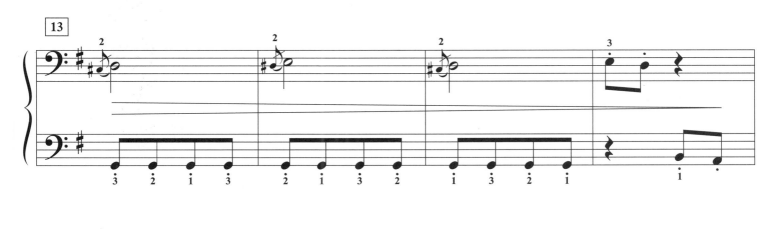

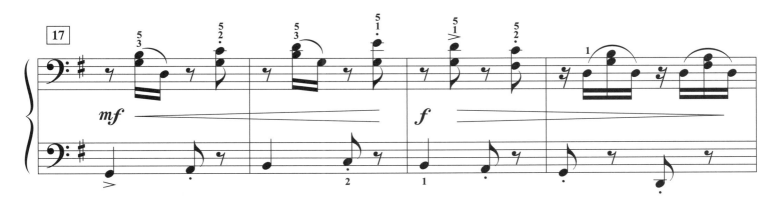

* m. 13-15 Use any L.H. fingering that is comfortable.

After playing, ask yourself:
- Which kind of touch releases did I use?

FJH2178

51

When playing:

• Use a rebound staccato touch release for all staccato ♩ notes.

Grandmama's Waltz

Opus 210, No. 12

by Louis Köhler
1820-1886, Germany

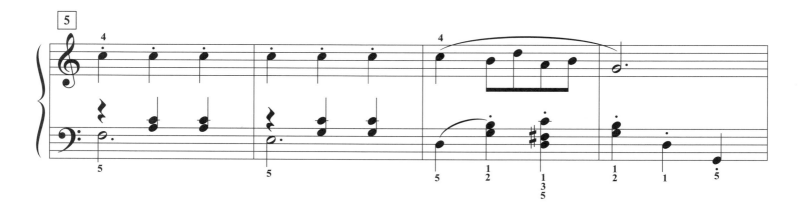

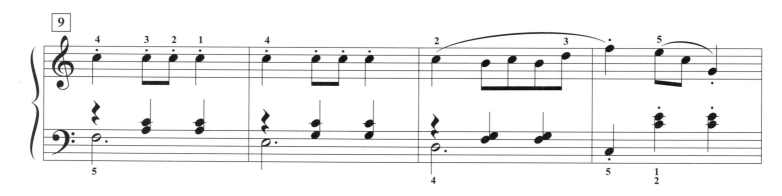

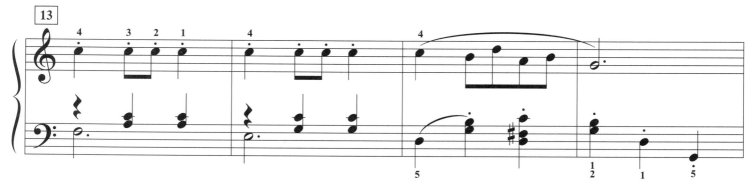

FJH2178

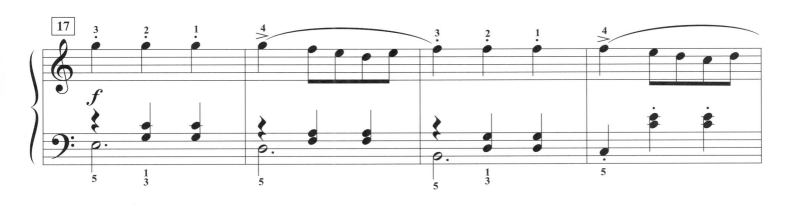

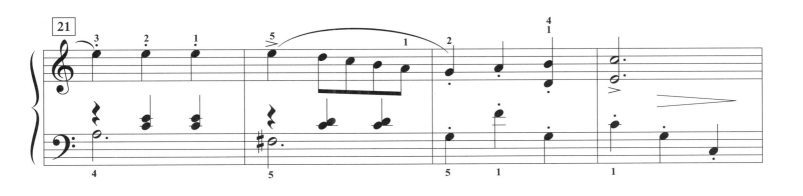

Before playing:

• Feel the natural accents on the main beats in each measure:

Jack Frost is an imaginary sprite who is responsible for cold and frosty weather, and for the fernlike patterns on cold windows in winter. Sometimes he "nips" at your nose when it's very cold outside. Usually he is carefree and happy and loves it when people play in the snow.

Jack Frost

(Op. 64, adapted)

by Jean Louis Gobbaerts (aka Streabbog), 1835-1886, Belgium

Arranged by Edwin McLean

CD 51/52 • MIDI 30

FJH2178

UNIT 9

Technique with Beethoven

1. **The Key of E♭ Major**
- Notice which finger begins and ends the scale.
- Notice the "3-4" finger combinations.

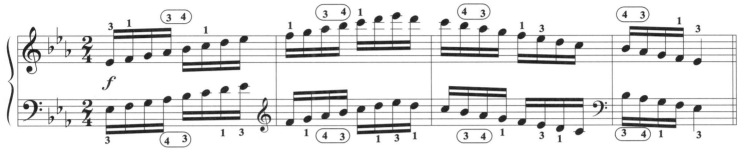

2. Now play the E♭ major cadence, triads and inversions, and arpeggio.

Here is the arpeggio:

3. ♩ = 60, ♩ = 72, ♩ = _____.
your choice

Carl Czerny, No. 84

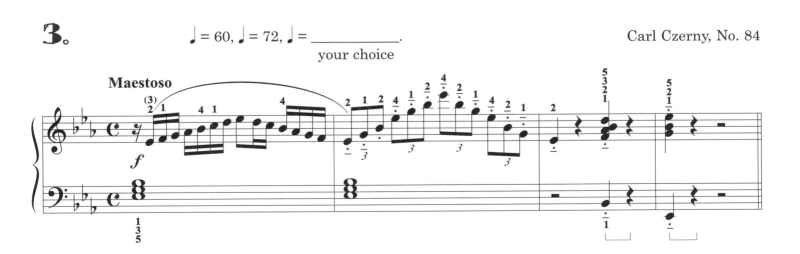

Air

by Wolfgang Amadeus Mozart
1756-1791, Austria

Assymetrical Rhythms and Changing Time Signatures

- An assymetrical rhythm is one that has an odd number at the top such as $\frac{5}{4}$, $\frac{7}{4}$.

1. Tap the following pattern with your teacher. Notice that in $\frac{5}{4}$ the pattern can be divided into two parts, with a natural accent on beats 1 and 3:

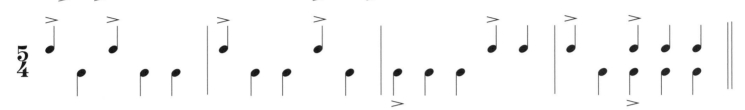

2. It's easy to count assymetrical rhythms when the ♩ remains steady.
Clap and count aloud (♩ = 100, ♩ = 132)

Now tap this example with changing time signatures and assymetrical rhythms:

Compound Meter and Changing Time Signatures

- In compound meter, the ♪ receives 1 beat and remains steady throughout.
Tap and count aloud (♪ = 112, ♪ = 160)

★ The piece on p.60-61 reinforces these new concepts.

rubato—For expressive purposes, a performer can take time (slow down). Shortly afterward, the time must be given back. Listen to the recording to hear this.

Deep River

Spiritual

Arranged by Edwin McLean

CD 56/57 • MIDI 33

Moderately slow; expressively ($\quarternote$ = ca. 92)

with rubato

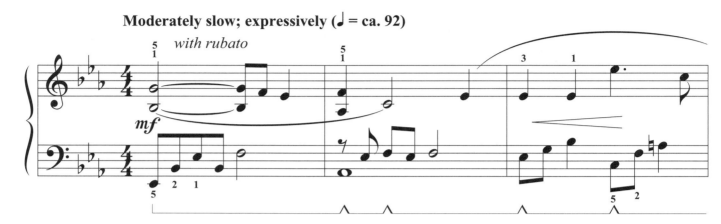

FJH2178

While playing:

· Use a *portato* touch release in this piece for a sustained sound.

Modest Mussorgsky (1839-1881) was a Russian composer. His best-known work is Pictures at an Exhibition, which is for solo piano. There is also a version for orchestra, orchestrated by Maurice Ravel. Mussorgsky, along with the composer Rimsky-Korsakov, formed a group called the Russian Five, who wrote music inspired by Russian history and folklore. Another famous piece of his is Night on Bald Mountain.

Promenade

from *Pictures at an Exhibition*
by Modest Petrovich Mussorgsky
1839-1881, Russia
Arranged by Timothy Brown

CD 58/59 • MIDI 34

FJH2178

CD 60 • MIDI 35

Technique with Liszt

1. **The Key of C Minor**
- C minor is the relative minor of E♭ major.
  (They are three half steps away from each other.)
- Like E♭ major, C minor has 3 flats (B♭, E♭, A♭).

2. **C Natural minor scale**
- Which note does your 4th finger play in the R.H.? _____ In the L.H.? _____
- C major and C minor have the same fingering.
- Practice hands alone, then hands together.

3. **Harmonic minor form** (raised 7th note ascending and descending)

4. **Melodic minor form** (raised 6th and 7th notes ascending and lowered on descending)

Liszt asks:
Can you play these scales as four-octave scales? Can you play them with the metronome with an even and beautiful sound?

FJH2178

5. Playing a C minor cadence

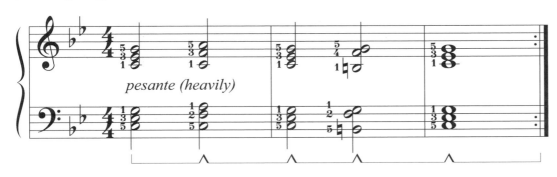

pesante (heavily)

Liszt says:
Say the name of the chords as you play!

6. Playing a two-octave arpeggio

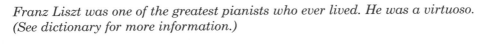

Franz Liszt was one of the greatest pianists who ever lived. He was a virtuoso.
(See dictionary for more information.)

Liszt says:
Remember that **parallel keys** share the same tonic note. For example, you can practice these exercises in C Major and then in C minor, and you will be playing in parallel keys.

Variations on Reuben and Rachel

by Kevin Olson

With energy (♩ = ca. 104)

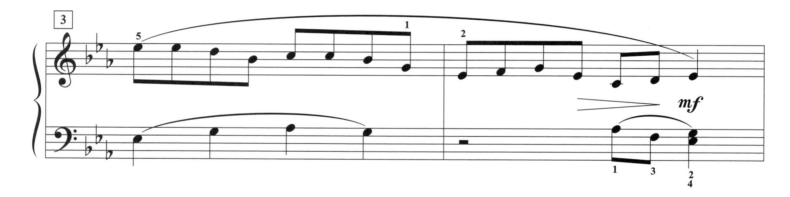

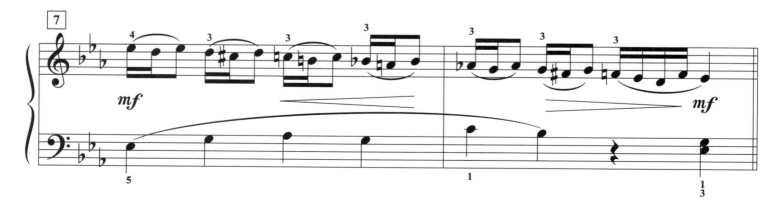

FJH2178

What is a Ballade?

The piece below is an example of a ballade.

Ballades have been around for centuries. Each one tells a story. If you want to say the word aloud, it's pronounced "ba-LAHD." The piece below is an example of a ballade.

First, practice the piece without the L.H. crossover notes. Then add the L.H. crossovers and pedal.

What do you think the story could be about? Play it in two tempi, first *tranquillo* (tranquil, calm), ♩= 84 and then *agitato* (agitated, excited). ♩= 112 How did the interpretations of your stories change with the two different tempi?

Suspense
by Helen Marlais

Listen to the CD recording of the famous ballade on the next page. What do you think this story is about? Create a story in your own mind, and then write a few words in the different sections of the piece so that you remember what it is all about. Putting stories to your music will help the music come alive when you are practicing and performing.

FJH2178

Ballade

Opus 100, No. 15

by Johann Friedrich Burgmüller
1806-1874, Germany

* *martellato* - a forceful, detached touch.

FJH2178

Music Dictionary
Tempo Markings

largo - slow and dignified   *adagio* - slowly   *andante* - walking speed
andantino - a little faster than *andante*   *allegretto* - a little slower than *allegro*
moderato - moderate speed   *allegro* - happy, spirited   *con brio* - with spirit or vigor
spiritoso - with spirit   *vivo* - with life   *vivace* - very quickly

Music term	Definition	Found on page:
a piacere	(Italian, pronounced "ah-pyah-CHAY-ray") "At pleasure," especially with regard to tempo and rhythm	5
accelerando	(Italian, pronounced "ah-chel-er-AHN-doh") Becoming faster	9
agitato	(Italian, pronounced "ah-jee-TAH-toh") Agitated, excited	66
Air	In Mozart's time, an Air referred to a piece with a beautiful melody and simple harmony	56
animato	(Italian, pronounced "ah-nee-MAH-toh") Animated, lively	68
appoggiatura	(Italian, pronounced "ahp-pah-jah-TOO-rah") An ornament that takes time from the second note, is played on the beat, and is louder than the note it resolves to. This is an expressive ornament. Don't confuse this ornament with the grace note, played *before* the beat	18
assymetrical rhythm	When a rhythmic pattern can be divided into two assymetrical (uneven) parts, with a natural accent that divides the rhythm pattern For example, $\frac{5}{4}$ can be divided into 3+2, or 2+3; $\frac{7}{4}$ can be divided into 2+2+3, or 3+2+2. Other examples are $\frac{5}{8}$ and $\frac{7}{8}$	57
augmented triad	When the top note of a major triad is raised by one half step. Remember that a diminished triad is a minor triad with a lowered fifth note	10
ballade	(French, pronounced "ba-LAHD") A ballade tells a story. Vocal ballades originated in the 1400s in France. The famous composer and pianist Chopin wrote four fabulous ballades for advanced pianists	66
double flat	Lowers a tone by two half steps. For example, in a C diminished 7th chord, the top note is a B double flat (not an A) so as to keep the order of notes as thirds apart from each other (C E♭ G♭ B♭♭). A double sharp raises a tone by two half steps	31
finger independence	A technique that is needed when one hand has to play two lines of music	16
grazioso	(Italian, pronounced "grah-tsee-OH-soh") Gracefully	12
leggero	(Italian, pronounced "lay-JAY-roh") Light, nimble	8
maestoso	(Italian, pronounced "mah-es-TOH-soh") With majesty	55
marcato	(Italian, pronounced "mahr-KAH-toh") Marked, stressed	40
martellato	(Italian, pronounced "mar-tel-LAH-toh") A forceful, detached touch	67

meno	(Italian, pronounced "MEH-noh") Less. The opposite is *più,* meaning more	33
mordent	This ornament adds brilliance to the melodic line. It is always played on the beat and goes down and then back up to the principal note	20
parallel keys	A major and minor scale which share the same tonic note. For example, D major and D minor are parallel keys	63
più mosso	(Italian, pronounced "pew-MOH-so") A little more motion	8
portato	(Italian, pronounced "pohr-TAH-toh") Halfway between *legato* and *staccato.* Think of it as a "sticky" touch	31
risoluto	(Italian, pronounced "ree-soh-LOO-toh") Bold, resolved	8
rubato	(Italian, pronounced "roo-BAH-toh") From the Italian word, *rubare,* which means "to rob." Subtle variations in tempo for expressive purposes. When the performer takes away time (slows down), it is made up shortly after	58
scherzando	(Italian, pronounced "skehr-TSAHN-doh") Joke-like	14
sequence	A phrase which is immediately repeated at a different pitch, usually one step lower or higher	40
seventh chords	There are many different kinds of seventh chords:	31

dominant 7th: minor 7th: diminished 7th: Major 7th:

sfz, sf, fz, (*sforzando*)	(Italian, pronounced "sfohr-TSAHN-doh") "Forcing"—a sudden strong accent	30
sonatina	A "little sonata." Comprised of three distinct parts—the exposition, development, and recapitulation	22
sostenuto	(Italian, pronounced "sohs-teh-NOO-toh") Sustained	15
spiritoso	(Italian, pronounced "spee-ree-TOH-soh") Spirited	4
toccatina	A little "toccata," which is a virtuoso keyboard composition with brilliant passagework in free style	40
tremolo	Rapidly playing notes back and forth for a prolonged sound	5
tranquillo	(Italian, pronounced "trahn-KWEEL-loh") Tranquil, calm	35
trill (*tr*) ⁓	A kind of ornamentation, which is used to embellish a cadence or specific notes within a work. It is a rapid alternation between two notes next to each other. In the Baroque era, trills usually begin on the note *above* the principal note and are played **on** the beat	21
virtuoso	Someone who has outstanding technical ability. Liszt, Rubinstein, Horowitz, and Rachmaninoff are examples of virtuoso pianists	50
vivo	(Italian, pronounced "VEE-voh") Brisk, lively	4
voicing	To bring out a melody over an accompaniment or to bring out the top note of a chord	6

Certificate of Achievement

Congratulations

_____

Student

has completed

Helen Marlais'
Succeeding at the Piano®

You can use the following repertoire in your future studies:

Succeeding with the Masters®, Volume One; Baroque, Classical, and Romantic Eras
The Festival Collection®, Books 3 and 4
Succeeding with the Masters® & The Festival Collection®, Etudes with Technique, Books 3 and 4
Succeeding with the Masters®—Sonatinas, Books 3 and 4
In Recital®, Book 4 and 5
The FJH Contemporary Keyboard Editions

For Technique:
Play Your Scales and Chords Every Day®, Books 5, 6, and 7
Energize Your Fingers Every Day™, Book 5

For Theory:
Write, Play, and Hear Your Theory Every Day®, Book 5

For Sight Reading:
Sight Reading & Rhythm Every Day®, Books 4A, 4B, and 5

_____   _____
Date   Teacher's Signature

THE
F·J·H
MUSIC
COMPANY
INC.
Frank J. Hackinson